Our Life in the Church

Activity Book

Our Life in the Church
Activity Book

Faith and Life Series
Third Edition

BOOK EIGHT

Ignatius Press, San Francisco
Catholics United for the Faith, Steubenville, Ohio

Director of First Edition: The late Rev. Msgr. Eugene Kevane, Ph.D.
Assistant Director and General Editor of First Edition: Patricia Puccetti Donahoe, M.A.
First Edition Writer: David R. Previtali

Revision Writer: Colette Ellis, M.A.
Revision Editors: Caroline Avakoff, M.A. and Matthew Ramsay
Revision Artist: Christopher J. Pelicano

Catholics United for the Faith, Inc. and Ignatius Press gratefully acknowledge the guidance and assistance of the late Reverend Monsignor Eugene Kevane, former Director of the Pontifical Catechetical Institute, Diocese of Arlington, Virginia, in the production of the First Edition of this series. The First Edition intended to implement the authentic approach in Catholic catechesis given to the Church through documents of the Holy See and in particular the Conference of Joseph Cardinal Ratzinger on "Sources and Transmission of Faith." The Revised Edition and Third Edition continue this commitment by drawing upon the *Catechism of the Catholic Church* (Libreria Editrice Vaticana, © 1994, 1997).

2015 reprint
See www.faithandlifeseries.com
for additional tools and resources
© 1987, 2005, 2011 Catholics United for the Faith, Inc.
All rights reserved
ISBN 978-1-58617-578-8
Manufactured by Friesens Corporation
Manufactured in Altona, MB, Canada in February 2015
Job # 210667
in compliance with the
Consumer Protection Safety Act

Contents

Dear Student,

As you learn the Faith during this school year, you will read from the *Faith and Life* student text, which focuses on the Church in the world. You will learn about the nature and structure of the Church, its history, its saints, and your possible vocation within the Church. Your teacher will help you to understand all that you have read.

This activity book is an opportunity for you to reflect on what you have learned each week. You will find various activities to help in this task. As you work on these activities in class or at home, you should think about what you read and discussed in class. Take the time to pray before and after the activities, and be sure to ask your teacher or your parents any questions that you might have.

It is our sincere hope that these activities, combined with the readings from each week, will help you to come to know Jesus Christ and to live an abundant life with him in the Church.

Name:_____

Christ's Abiding Presence

Answer the following questions in complete sentences.

1. How much does Jesus love us?

2. What did he mean when he said he will not leave us orphans?

3. Who did Jesus and God the Father send to us?

4. Why did Christ found a Church?

5. What does it mean for you to be a member of Christ's Church?

Name:_____

The Church of Christ

Answer the following questions in complete sentences.

1. Read Matthew 16:16–19 in which Jesus says he will build his Church. What do we know about the Church from this passage?

2. What role would Peter have in this Church?

3. Why do you think Jesus gave his authority to Peter in front of the other Apostles?

4. In Matthew 18:17, Jesus speaks again of his Church. What role will the Church have according to this passage?

5. Is the Church merely a human institution?

6. Is the Church only divine?

Name:_____

Church Structure

Using the analogy of an orchestra, explain the structure of the Church.

_____

_____

_____

_____

_____

_____

_____

_____

_____

_____

_____

_____

_____

_____

_____

_____

_____

_____

_____

_____

_____

_____

_____

Name:_____

Understanding Christ's Church

Read the following Bible verses and write a brief paragraph on what they teach us about the Church.

1 Corinthians 12:27—13:13

Ephesians 5:21–33

Name:_____

The Birth of the Church

Answer the following questions in complete sentences.

1. What did Jesus promise during his last discourse?

2. Who gives life to the Church?

3. Explain why Pentecost is called the "birthday" of the Church?

4. What grace did the Holy Spirit give the followers of Jesus who gathered in the upper room?

5. Was Pentecost the beginning of God's plan for the Church? Explain your answer.

6. Read all of Acts 2 and write what happened after the descent of the Holy Spirit.

Name:_____

The Church in God's Plan

Answer the following questions in complete sentences.

1. Write about God's plan for the Church through the Old Testament in the events of the following people's lives.

   Adam and Eve:

   Noah (see Gen 6:1—9:11):

   Abraham:

   Moses:

   David:

2. Define the Greek word *ekklesia* and explain how it relates to the Church.

Name:_____

Jesus Founds the Church

Answer the following questions in complete sentences.

1. Briefly explain how God established the Church during each of the three stages listed below:

    How was the Church prefigured in the Old Testament?

    How did Christ form the Church?

    How is the Church manifested to the world?

2. Explain the deposit of grace. How do we receive it?

3. Explain the deposit of Faith. How was it handed on?

Name:_____

Fishers of Men

Write a brief essay on what Jesus meant when he called his Apostles to be "fishers of men." How can you be a fisher of men, too?

_____

_____

_____

_____

_____

_____

_____

_____

_____

_____

_____

_____

_____

_____

_____

_____

_____

_____

_____

_____

_____

Name:_____

Creation

Explain the following images of the Church.

Kingdom (Jn 14:2; Mt 3:2; 5:1–12):

Mustard Seed (Mk 4:30–32):

Vineyard (Mt 21:33–43):

Sheepfold (Jn 10:1–10):

Treasure (Mt 6:21; 13:44):

Net (Mt 13:47):

Bride (Rev 21:9; 19:7; 22:17; Eph 5:23–33):

Mystical Body (1 Cor 12:12–31):

The Marks of the Church I

Explain the following marks of the Church.

The Church is One:

_____

_____

_____

_____

_____

_____

_____

_____

_____

The Church is Holy:

_____

_____

_____

_____

_____

_____

_____

_____

_____

_____

_____

Name:_____

The Marks of the Church II

Explain the following marks of the Church.

The Church is Catholic:

_____

_____

_____

_____

_____

_____

_____

_____

_____

_____

_____

The Church is Apostolic:

_____

_____

_____

_____

_____

_____

_____

_____

_____

_____

_____

Name:_____

Why the Church?

Answer the following questions in complete sentences and find Bible passages to support your answers.

1. Why did Jesus Christ found the Church?

2. What did Jesus entrust to Peter and the Apostles?

3. What did Jesus give the Church in order to continue his work?

4. What power did the Apostles receive at the Last Supper?

5. What power did the Apostles receive after the Resurrection?

6. What were they commanded to do on the day of the Ascension?

Name:_____

Revelation

Answer the following questions in complete sentences.

1. Who comprises the living voice of the Church?

2. What is revelation?

3. When did public revelation begin and end?

4. Who is the source of revelation?

5. In what two ways is the Word of God passed on to us?

6. What is Sacred Tradition?

7. What is Sacred Scripture?

Name:_____

Creeds and Councils

Answer the following questions in complete sentences.

1. What is a creed?

2. What is the Apostles' Creed?

3. What is the Nicene Creed?

4. Why were creeds written?

5. What is an ecumenical council?

6. What is discussed at ecumenical councils?

Name: _____

Our Heritage of Faith

Write descriptions of the Fathers and Doctors of the Church below:

Fathers of the Church:

_____

_____

_____

_____

_____

_____

_____

_____

_____

_____

_____

Doctors of the Church:

_____

_____

_____

_____

_____

_____

_____

_____

_____

_____

_____

_____

Name:_____

Development of Doctrine

Answer the following questions in complete sentences.

1. What is *sensus fidelium*?

2. What is *sensus fidei*?

3. What are encyclicals?

4. Explain the development of doctrine. Do the truths of the Church change?

5. Using the example of the Immaculate Conception, explain the process of the development of doctrine?

Name:_____

Authority in the Church

Answer the following questions in complete sentences.

1. What kind of authority did Christ give
   to his Apostles?

2. What did Jesus commission his Apostles
   to do?

3. Who forms the hierarchy of the Church?

4. Who is the Pope? What is Papal Primacy?

5. How is he *Servus servorum Dei*?

6. Who are the bishops?

Name:_____

Free from Error

Answer the following questions in complete sentences.

1. Why is it so important that Church teachings remain free from error?

2. What is infallibility?

3. Does obedience to Church authority make one more or less free? Explain.

Name:_____

Magisterium

Answer the following questions in complete sentences.

1. Explain the following:

    Extraordinary Magisterium:

    Ordinary Magisterium:

2. Define the following words.

    Ex cathedra:

    Synod:

    Magisterium:

3. Write a paragraph on the infallibility of the Pope. Include the four conditions an infallible papal teaching must have.

Name:_____

The Church Governs

Answer the following questions in complete sentences.

1. What are doctrines of our Faith?

2. How does the Church exercise her authority in discipline?

3. Why do we follow the Church's rule on fasting?

4. What are other examples of Church authority in discipline?

5. What is obedience?

6. How must the faithful in the Church act like players on a football team?

Name:_____

Successors of the Apostles

Answer the following questions in complete sentences.

1. Who did Jesus establish as the head of his Church?

2. What role did the other Apostles have in the hierarchy of the Church?

3. How did St. Peter know that he was to choose a successor for Judas?

4. Why did Jesus establish a hierarchical structure for his Church?

5. Compare the structure of the Church with the structure of the Jewish religion in the Old Testament.

6. Is the Church human? Is the Church supernatural?

7. How did the authority of the Apostles get passed on to other bishops, including our bishops today?

Name:_____

Church Structure from the Bible

Read the following Bible verses and write a brief paragraph about the institution of Church structure.

Matthew 13:16–17; 16:13–20:

_____

_____

_____

_____

_____

_____

_____

_____

_____

_____

Acts 6:2–6; 15:1–35:

_____

_____

_____

_____

_____

_____

_____

_____

_____

_____

_____

Name:_____

Worldwide Organization of the Church

Answer the following questions in complete sentences.

1. What is a diocese? What is your diocese?

2. Who is the head of each diocese and what is his role?

3. What powers does the bishop give to priests and deacons? How do they share in his teaching office?

4. What is a parish? What is a pastor?

5. What is a parishioner?

6. What is a monsignor? What is a cardinal?

7. What is the Roman curia?

Name:_____

Visible Church Hierarchy

Complete the crossword puzzle using the clues below.

In founding his Church, Our Lord accomplished the fulfillment of the (9 down) Testament. He gave (7 across) to his Apostles, declaring that sins which were forgiven on (2 down) would be forgiven in (1 across) . In the (15 down) , we read that the Apostles selected successors, the bishops, to carry on Christ's (16 across) .

Today the Holy Father leads the Church in union with the bishops of the world and is assisted by the cardinals, some of whom help in the (5 down).

The bishops, as shepherds, (8 down) , govern, and (17 across) the people. To assist them in these tasks, they confer (12 across) on (6 down) and (10 across) through the Sacrament of Holy (11 down) , each according to his own particular (3 across) in the Body of Christ.

Pastors perform their priestly duties in the (14 across) community. Deacons serve the People of God by preaching and performing Works of (13 down) . (4 down) people are also called to participate in the evangelical mission of the Church in their families, work places, and neighborhoods.

Name:_____

Baptism

Write an essay summarizing the Church's teaching on Baptism. Be sure to include whether we must be baptized in order to be saved and enter heaven.

Name:_____

The Divinity of Jesus

Using your student text and the Catechism of the Catholic Church, paragraphs 1328–1332, explain how the Eucharist is:

1. A meal:

2. A sacrifice:

3. A communion:

4. A holy and divine liturgy, the greatest act of worship:

5. A memorial:

6. The Holy Mass:

7. Jesus:

Name:_____

Confirmation

Answer the following questions in complete sentences.

1. Why do we need Confirmation if we receive the Holy Spirit at Baptism?

2 .What responsibilities do you take on in the Church when you are confirmed?

3. What does it mean to be a "soldier of Christ"? What does St. Paul say is the armor of God?

4. How can we continue to strengthen our faith?

5. Unscramble the names of the gifts and fruits of the Holy Spirit. Underline the gifts and circle the fruits.

OYJ	TDYEOSM
EEPAC	GELDKONWE
RREEAFFOHTLDO	ERTEGNIYSO
ITYPE	TAPIEENC
HSCATITY	GOSOSDEN
HAIRTCY	CTFEOONSLLR
DUNRETNGDASNI	NGELSTSENE
WMISDO	TITORFUDE
SSKNDEIN	LFTINSFUASEH
NOUSCEL	

Name:_____

Different Rites

I. Compare the Roman and the Byzantine rites in the chart below.

ROMAN RITE	BYZANTINE

II. Answer the following questions in complete sentences.

1. Where did the different rites come from?

2. Do all rites share the same essential teachings?

3. Do all the various Catholic rites have the same Pope?

Name:_____

Worship

Answer the following questions in complete sentences.

1. What does "liturgy" mean?

2. How does the liturgy differ from private devotions?

3. Why is it proper that the Church as a people should join Christ in the liturgy in his priestly role of giving honor and praise to God?

4. What are the three elements to liturgy? Explain them.
    1.

    2.

    3.

5. How can the liturgy be a sign of the unity of the Church?

6. Why do we have rituals?

Name:_____

Liturgical Year

Make a pie chart of the liturgical year. Use the proper liturgical colors.

Compare the liturgical year to the natural (seasonal) year.

_____
_____
_____
_____
_____
_____
_____
_____
_____
_____

Name:_____

Liturgical Seasons: Christmas and Easter

Answer the following questions in complete sentences.

1. What are we preparing for during Advent?

2. Why is Advent a season of penance?

3. When does the Christmas season begin and end?

4. What do we celebrate during Christmas?

5. What do the forty days of Lent represent?

6. During Lent, what does the Church urge us to do?

7. What is special about Holy Week?

8. When does Easter season begin?

9. How long is the Easter season?

Name:_____

Ordinary Time and Feast Days

Answer the following questions in complete sentences.

1. What is Pentecost and when is it celebrated during the liturgical year?

2. When is ordinary time?

3. What does the Church reflect upon during ordinary time?

4. List the liturgical colors and what they symbolize.

5. Into what three main groups can we divide the other feasts that occur during the liturgical year? For each group, explain what they are and give some examples.
    1.

    2.

    3.

Mary: Mother of the Church

Answer the following questions in complete sentences.

1. Why does Mary have an important role in salvation?

2. What is the Annunciation?

In the chart below, compare Mary and Eve. Remember that Mary is the New Eve.

EVE	MARY
Made without Original Sin	
Received life from the rib of Adam	
Had sanctifying grace	
God asked something of her	
Eve listened to the voice of the angel of lies	
Eve disobeyed God and offered the forbidden fruit to Adam	
Sin, death, darkness, and all the effects of sin entered the world	
A woman and her seed were promised to redeem the world	
Called Mother of the Living	

Name:_____

Free from Original Sin

Answer the following questions in complete sentences.

1. What is Original Sin, who has it, and what does it do to our souls?

2. Why does Mary not have Original Sin and what is this great privilege called?

3. When was this doctrine infallibly defined? By whom?

4. How did Mary confirm this doctrine?

5. When do we celebrate this mystery and feast?

Name:_____

More Privileges of Mary

Answer the following questions in complete sentences.

1. What is Mary's perpetual virginity?

2. How do we know that St. Joseph is not Jesus' father?

3. Which creeds teach Mary's perpetual virginity?

4. What is the Assumption of Mary?

5. When was the doctrine of the Assumption declared infallibly?

6. When do we celebrate this feast?

Mary in our Lives

Answer the following questions in complete sentences.

1. Why is Mary Queen of the angels and saints (and heaven and earth!)?

2. What does veneration mean, and why does Mary receive it from us?

3. What did Pope St. Pius X say about Mary?

4. How does Mary help us on our way to Christ?

5. What does it mean for Mary to intercede for us?

6. What is the Litany of Loreto? Explain this prayer.

Name:_____

The Church Militant

Answer the following questions in complete sentences.

1. What is the Church Militant?

2. What is the Church Militant fighting?

3. How is the Church Militant united in love?

4. How do we partake in intercessory prayer?

Name:_____

The Church Suffering

Answer the following questions in complete sentences.

1. What is the Church Suffering?

2. Who goes to purgatory? Why? What happens there?

3. What does Matthew 22:2–12 teach us about purgatory?

4. What is the principal suffering in purgatory? Are the souls also full of peace? Why?

5. Can souls in purgatory help themselves? Discuss a passage from the Bible that tells us what we should do for the Church Suffering.

6. When do we pray for the dead during the liturgy? What else can we do to help the souls in purgatory?

Name:_____

The Church Triumphant

Answer the following questions in complete sentences.

1. What is the Church Triumphant?

2. Who are the canonized saints?

3. How do we honor the Church Triumphant during the liturgy?

4. How are we united with them?

5. How can we turn to the saints for help?

6. When we venerate the saints, do we also honor God? Why?

7. When did the Church start devotion to the saints?

Name:_____

Definitions

Define the following words using the student text.

Communion of Saints:

Church Triumphant:

Church Suffering:

Pilgrim Church:

Church Militant:

Intercessory Prayer:

Canonized Saint:

Mystical Body of Christ:

All Souls' Day:

All Saints' Day:

Name:_____

Apostles and Martyrs

Answer the following questions in complete sentences.

1. What happened in the early days of the Church?

2. What happened to St. Peter?

3. Who was the greatest missionary in the early Church? What did he do?

4. What characterized the next 250 years of the Church? Who are the martyrs?

5. How is it that the "blood of the martyrs is the seed of the Church"?

6. How did Ss. Perpetua and Felicity witness to their Faith?

Name:_____

Fathers and Doctors of the Church

Answer the following questions in complete sentences.

1. When and why did the age of martyrdom end?

2. What is heresy? What is a heretic?

3. What is Arianism? When was it denounced?

4. Who is St. Athanasius? What is his significance in the Church?

5. Who is St. Augustine? What is his significance in the Church?

Name:_____

Monasteries

Answer the following questions in complete sentences.

1. What happened in the fifth century and how did the Church respond?

2. How did monasteries, with monks and monastic rules, help the Church face this challenge?

3. Who is St. Benedict and what is his importance to the Church?

4. Who is St. Columban and what is his importance to the Church?

Name:_____

The Church Faces Problems

Answer the following questions in complete sentences.

1. What is Islam?

2. How did Muslims separate the East from the West and how did this separation contribute to the schism in 1054?

3. Explain the great problem that faced the Church from within, near the end of her first thousand years.

4. Did the Holy Spirit abandon the Church during those years? How can we say the Church is divine when corruption occurs in the Church?

Name:_____

The Crusades

Answer the following questions in complete sentences.

1. Who is St. Bernard of Clairvaux? What is his importance to the Church?

2. What were the Crusades and why were they waged?

3. Who is King Louis IX and what is his importance in the Church?

4. Did the Crusaders win the war?

5. What was the effect of the Crusades?

Name:_____

The Middle Ages

Answer the following questions in complete sentences.

1. What two new religious orders were founded during the Middle Ages and how did they differ from monastic orders?

2. Who is St. Francis of Assisi and what is his importance to the Church?

3. Who is St. Dominic de Guzman and what is his importance to the Church?

4. Who is St. Thomas Aquinas and what is his importance to the Church?

5. Who is St. Catherine of Siena and what is her importance to the Church?

Name:_____

The Protestant Reformation

Answer the following questions in complete sentences.

1. What is the Protestant Reformation? How did Martin Luther contribute to it?

2. What is the Council of Trent? Why was this council called?

3. What is the Counter-Reformation?

4. List two important religious orders that helped renew the Church during the Counter-Reformation.

5. Who is St. Ignatius of Loyola and what is his importance to the Church?

6. Who were some of the missionaries to the New World and what did they do?

Name:_____

Modern Times

Answer the following questions in complete sentences.

1. What are the teachings of Modernism?

2. Who is Pope St. Pius X and what is his importance to the Church?

3. What is one of the main challenges that the Church and the world have faced in modern times?

4. Who is St. Maximilian Kolbe and what is his importance to the Church?

Name:_____

Separated Brethren: Orthodox and Protestants

Answer the following questions in complete sentences.

1. Are baptized non-Catholics part of the Mystical Body of Christ? Explain.

2. What is the only religion that teaches the full message of Our Lord? Do other religions have elements of truth and holiness?

3. How do Orthodox Christians differ from us? What do we have in common?

4. How do the churches that broke away from us in the Reformation relate to the Catholic Church? (What are their similarities? What are their differences?)

Name:_____

Jews

Answer the following questions in complete sentences.

1. Who are the Jews?

2. Explain how the Jews bear a close relationship with the Church and how we are united with them by a special bond.

3. What did God gradually reveal to the Jews?

4. Did the Jews recognize Jesus as the Messiah? List some reasons why or why not.

5. Why do we pray that they will "arrive at the fullness of redemption"?

Name:_____

Muslims

Answer the following questions in complete sentences.

1. Do the Muslims believe in one God?

2. How does Islam differ from Judaism?

3. When did Islam begin?

4. Do Muslims recognize Jesus Christ as the Son of God?

Name:_____

Pagans and Atheists

Answer the following questions in complete sentences.

1. What do pagans and atheists have in common?

2. What are the pagan practices of polytheism and animism?

3. What three ways do modern men deny the existence of God?

4. Explain the phrase: "Outside the Church there is no salvation."

Name:_____

Call to Holiness

Answer the following questions in complete sentences.

1. What does it mean to say that each
   Christian is called to holiness?

2. What is an apostolate?

3. What is a specific vocation?

4. After Baptism and the removal of Original Sin, what obstacles to holiness
   remain?

5. Define vice and explain how we acquire it.

6. How can what we know about vice help us to grow in holiness?

Name:_____

Seven Capital Sins: Pride and Covetousness

Answer the following questions in complete sentences.

1. What is pride?

2. Why is pride the chief capital sin?

3. How was pride at the root of the sin of our first parents?

4. What is rightful pride?

5. What is covetousness?

6. If material things are good, why is covetousness wrong?

7. How can covetousness lead to other sins?

Seven Capital Sins: Lust and Anger

Answer the following questions in complete sentences.

1. What is lust?

2. When is attraction to the oppostie sex healthy and good?

3. When does sexual pleasure become disordered?

4. What is anger?

5. What is righteous anger? How does this differ from sinful anger?

Name:_____

Seven Capital Sins: Gluttony, Envy, and Sloth

Answer the following questions in complete sentences.

1. What is gluttony?

2. When is our desire for food good? When does it become disordered?

3. What is envy?

4. Is any act of wishing to be like another a sin of envy? Explain.

5. What is sloth and how is it unlike the other vices?

6. How does a desire for rest and leisure become disordered?

Name:_____

The Life of Virtue

Answer the following questions in complete sentences.

1. What is a virtue?

2. List the two types of virtues and explain how they are acquired.

3. How does growing in virtue compare to being a runner?

4. Are virtues easy? Should we find joy in living them?

5. Compare the pleasure of a life of virtue with the "pleasure" of a life of vice.

Name:_____

The Cardinal Virtues

I. Answer the following questions in complete sentences.

1. What are the chief moral virtues?

2. Why are the chief moral virtues called "cardinal" virtues?

II. In the chart below, explain and give examples of the cardinal virtues.

VIRTUE	EXPLANATION AND EXAMPLE
Prudence	
Justice	
Fortitude	
Temperance	

Name: _____

Other Moral Virtues

For each of the following virtues, give a definition, an example, and the name of the capital sin they counter.

VIRTUE	EXPLANATION AND EXAMPLE
Humility	
Liberality	
Chastity	
Meekness	
Moderation and Sobriety	
Brotherly Love	
Diligence	

Name:_____

The Theological Virtues

I. Answer the following question in complete sentences.

1. What are the supernatural theological virtues?

2. When do we receive them?

3. How do we exercise them?

4. Why are they called "theological" virtues?

II. In the chart below, explain the theological virtues.

VIRTUE	EXPLANATION
Faith	
Hope	
Love	

Name:_____

Works of Mercy

Answer the following questions in complete sentences.

1. How do the Works of Mercy help us to grow in virtue?

2. Why are there both Spiritual and Corporal Works of Mercy?

3. Why are the Spiritual Works of Mercy most important?

4. What are we preparing for by living the virtuous life and practicing the Works of Mercy?

5. What kind of happiness does a virtuous life lead to?

Name:_____

Spiritual Works of Mercy

Explain each Spiritual Work of Mercy.

WORK OF MERCY	EXPLANATION
Admonish the sinner	
Instruct the ignorant	
Counsel the doubtful	
Comfort the sorrow-ful	
Bear wrongs patiently	
Forgive all injuries	
Pray for the living and the dead	

Name:_____

Corporal Works of Mercy

Explain each Corporal Work of Mercy.

WORK OF MERCY	EXPLANATION
Feed the hungry	
Give drink to the thirsty	
Clothe the naked	
Visit the imprisoned	
Shelter the homeless	
Visit the sick	
Bury the dead	

Name:_____

Beatitudes

Answer the following questions in complete sentences.

1. Write the Beatitudes found in Matthew 5:3–11.

    1.

    2.

    3.

    4.

    5.

    6.

    7.

    8.

2. What happiness does Jesus promise to those who live the moral life?

3. Why does Jesus, contrary to the opinion of the world, call the person who is humble and suffers tribulations happy?

4. Can people be truly happy if they seek what the world promises will bring happiness?

Name:_____

Vocations

Answer the following questions in complete sentences.

1. What vocation do all of us share as Christians?

2. Why do we also have a particular call, or vocation?

Write a brief essay on why the call to religious life is the highest calling.
Discuss what Jesus asks of and promises to those who are called; how it allows
them to follow Christ more perfectly; and why, if this is objectively a higher call,
not everyone is called to it.

_____

_____

_____

_____

_____

_____

_____

_____

_____

_____

_____

_____

_____

_____

_____

Name:_____

Religious Life

Answer the following questions in complete sentences.

1. What are the evangelical counsels and why do religious vow to follow them?

2. What are vows?

3. Explain the vow of poverty.

4. Explain the vow of chastity.

5. Explain the vow of obedience.

6. Practicing the evangelical counsels is a way of imitiating Christ. Explain how Our Lord lived each of these counsels.

Name:_____

Religious Communities

In the chart below, compare contemplative and active religious communities using your text as a guide.

CONTEMPLATIVE	ACTIVE

Name:_____

Priesthood

Answer the following questions in complete sentences.

1. Can someone simply choose to become a priest? Explain.

2. Explain the call to Holy Orders?

3. How do those who have received Holy Orders minister grace and share in the redeeming work of Jesus Christ?

4. What are the three kinds of clergy?

5. What promises do Latin rite priests make?

Name:_____

The Lay Apostolate

Answer the following questions in complete sentences.

1. Who are the laity?

2. What call do the laity share in? How does this make them like those called to the religious life?

3. How is the vocation of the laity different from the vocation of the religious?

4. How can the laity's witness to the gospel sometimes be more effective than that of those who are in religious life?

5. What does it mean to live in the world, but not of the world? Give an example.

Name:_____

Sanctifying the World

Answer the following questions in complete sentences.

1. To what must the laity bring Christian justice and charity? Why?

2. What three goods are the laity especially called to use? Explain.

3. How is St. Paul's admonition in Romans 12:2 particularly important for the laity?

4. How can we sanctify our ordinary labor?

5. As students (who are laity), how can you sanctify your work?

6. As laity, how can you bring Christ's gospel message to the world and be his witness?

Name:_____

The Single Life

Answer the following questions in complete sentences.

1. What graces do those who live the single state receive?

2. How do both married and unmarried people live chastity?

3. In what state does everyone begin life? Why is this state important?

4. List some reasons why a lay person may remain unmarried?

Name:_____

In the World...

Explain how the laity can bring justice and charity to the following areas of human life.

Social:

Economic:

Industrial:

Political:

Cultural:

Recreational:

Educational:

Marriage and Family

Answer the following questions in complete sentences.

1. What are the vocations of love? To what kind of love is marriage ordered?

2. How are men and women different from everything else in the world that God created?

3. What does it mean for the family to be a community of love? Compare the family to the Blessed Trinity.

4. What did God command men and women?

5. What kind of community is formed in marriage?

Name:_____

Marriage: Husband and Wife

Answer the following questions in complete sentences.

1. What does Genesis 2:18 tell us about marriage?

2. Why are married couples called to sacrifice some of their individual freedom?

3. What does Genesis 2:22–24 tell us about marriage?

4. What is total self-giving?

5. Read Ephesians 5:21–33. Whom should we look to as a model for love and marriage?

Name:_____

The Sacrament of Marriage

Answer the following questions in complete sentences.

1. Since Creation, marriage has been a natural union between a man and a woman. How did it become a Sacrament?

2. What graces does Christ bestow on marriage?

3. What does it mean to say that the bearing and raising of children has been raised to a supernatural level?

4. What does mutual sanctification mean?

5. What does "indissoluble" mean? How did Jesus apply it to marriage?

Name:_____

The Family and Filial Piety

Answer the following questions in complete sentences.

1. Why is the family the basic unit of society?

2. What is the first obligation of the husband and wife?

3. What is the second obligation of parents?

4. What is the third obligation of parents? What is the most important part of this obligation?

5. What is the virtue of filial piety and why is it part of the virtue of justice?

6. What does filial piety require of us?

7. Other than their parents, whom must the children love and respect?

8. Why must you eventually take responsibility for your education in the Faith?

Name:_____

The Christian in the World

Answer the following questions in complete sentences.

1. What (or who) is the source of all authority?

2. What is the purpose of civil society?

3. What is the common good?

4. Who taught us the importance of recognizing civil authority? How did he do this?

5. What two sets of laws must we obey, and in what order?

6. What three things should the laws of society promote?

Name:_____

God's Laws Come First

Answer the following questions in complete sentences.

1. Why are we not bound to obey laws that contradict God's laws?

2. How is the state violating its authority if it demands something contrary to God's law?

3. Explain the difficulty St. Thomas More faced and how it led to his martyrdom. What can we learn from the stand he took?

Name:_____

Civil Laws

Answer the following questions in complete sentences.

1. Which civil laws are we bound to follow? Give an example of such a law.

2. What is patriotism?

3. How are excessive nationalism and treason disordered ways of loving one's country?

4. List and explain four of the duties we owe to our country as Christians.

5. Why and how must we work for the common good beyond our nation? Give some examples of this work from recent news.

Name:_____

The Christian View of Creatures

Answer the following questions in complete sentences.

1. Explain man's dominion over creation. What sort of rights and responsibilities does it give us?

2. How do we exercise stewardship over creation?

3. Give some examples of modern-day stewardship.

4. What can we learn from St. Francis of Assisi's love of nature?

Name: _____

Eternal Law

Write a brief essay about the two divisions of God's eternal law. Describe and give examples of each type of law, and answer the following questions: What is their purpose? Can they be disobeyed? Can they change?

Physical Laws:

_____

_____

_____

_____

_____

_____

_____

_____

_____

_____

Moral Laws:

_____

_____

_____

_____

_____

_____

_____

_____

_____

_____

Name:_____

Natural and Revealed Moral Law

Write a brief essay comparing natural and revealed moral law using the information given in your student text. Be sure to include the source of each and to explain why we need both.

Natural Law:

_____

_____

_____

_____

_____

_____

_____

_____

_____

_____

Revealed Law:

_____

_____

_____

_____

_____

_____

_____

_____

_____

_____

Name:_____

Ecclesiastical Laws

Answer the following questions in complete sentences.

1. What are the ecclesiastical laws, who makes them, and where are many of them found?

2. What are the precepts of the Church?

3. What are the "spirit" and the "letter" of the law?

4. What is legalism?

5. What law is supreme?

Name:_____

Conscience

Answer the following questions in complete sentences.

1. What is the conscience and what does it do?

2. Is the conscience in the intellect, will, or passions (emotions)? Explain.

3. Why is it so important that a conscience be correctly formed?

4. How can we properly form our conscience?

5. Explain the difference between true, false, lax, and scrupulous consciences.

Name:_____

The Church and the Social Order

Answer the following questions in complete sentences.

1. How does Jesus' last command to his Apostles require more than individual Baptisms?

2. What does it mean to form a Christian nation?

3. Which four sins cry out to heaven? What is significant about these four sins?

4. What are encyclicals and why are they important?

Name:_____

Protection of Human Life

Answer the following questions in complete sentences.

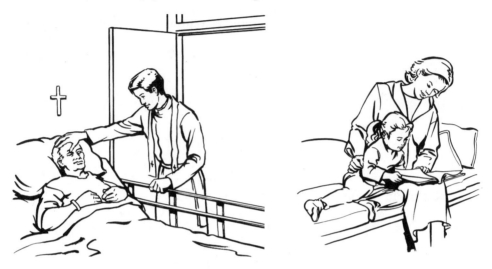

1. Is all killing necessarily wrong? Use the example of self-defense.

2. What is meant by the Fifth Commandment?

3. What is abortion? Is this always wrong?

4. Give the names and authors of three encyclicals which have defended the right to life.

Name:_____

War and Peace

Answer the following questions in complete sentences.

1. Can war ever be just? Explain.

2. Give the conditions for just war found in your student text.

    1.

    2.

    3.

    4.

3. What type of actions in war can never be just as taught by the Second Vatican Council?

4. How is unjust war contrary to God's plan?

Name:_____

Social Justice

Answer the following questions in complete sentences.

1. Define justice and social justice.

2. Which sins are fought against in the Church's economic teaching? Why?

3. What is a "fair wage" and why is it a matter of justice?

4. Name some encyclicals that have been written on social justice.

5. Why have certain forms of government been condemned by the Church?

Name:_____

Prayer

I. Answer the following questions in complete sentences.

1. What is prayer?

2. How do we know that prayer is essential to our spiritual lives?

3. What did Jesus teach about prayer in Luke 18:1?

4. How are we to deal with distractions in prayer?

II. In the chart below, explain the five steps to prayer and give examples of each.

STEP 1: PREPARE
STEP 2: BE HUMBLE
STEP 3: HAVE FAITH AND CONFIDENCE
STEP 4: PRAY WITH RESIGNATION
STEP 5: PRAY WITH PERSEVERANCE

Name:_____

Methods of Prayer

Answer the following questions in complete sentences.

1. What is mental prayer?

2. What is vocal prayer?

3. What is the difference between formal and informal vocal prayer?

4. Why is Mass the perfect prayer?

5. Why is the Liturgy of the Hours an important prayer?

Name:_____

Kinds of Prayer

There are many kinds of prayer. Give a description of the following four kinds of prayer and an example prayer that expresses each one.

ADORATION

THANKSGIVING

CONTRITION

PETITION

Name:_____

The Our Father

Write a meditation on the Our Father, or explain the prayer line by line.

Our Father, who art in heaven,

hallowed be thy name.

Thy Kingdom come.

Thy will be done

on earth, as it is in heaven.

Give us this day our daily bread,

and forgive us our trespasses, as we forgive those who trespass against us,

and lead us not into temptation,

but deliver us from evil.

AMEN.

Name:_____

The Sacramental Life

Answer the following questions in complete sentences.

1. Define Sacrament.

2. Who gave us the Sacraments and why did he give them to us?

3. What is the difference between a sign and an efficacious sign?

4. Why did Jesus give us the Sacraments as sensible means to receive his grace?

5. What do all the Sacraments do for us?

Name: _____

The Sacrament of Penance

Answer the following questions in complete sentences.

1. How did Jesus institute the Sacrament of Penance?

2. If Original Sin is removed in Baptism, why do we need the Sacrament of Penance?

3. What does God do for us in the Sacrament of Penance if we confess mortal sins we have committed?

4. What does God do for us in the Sacrament of Penance if we confess venial sins?

5. How do the sacramental graces we receive in the Sacrament of Penance help us?

Name:_____

Five Steps to a Good Confession

In the chart below, explain the five steps to a good Confession and why we must do each step.

1. Examination of Conscience
2. Contrition
3. Firm commitment not to sin again
4. Confess your sins
5. Perform the penance

Name:_____

The Sacrament of the Holy Eucharist

Answer the following questions in complete sentences.

1. What is the Eucharist?

2. Why do we call the Eucharist the source of grace?

3. Why do we call it our spiritual food?

4. Explain what happens to us when we receive the Eucharist and think about how it is truly a Holy Communion.

5. List and explain the four steps to a worthy reception of Holy Communion.

6. Choose one of the quotations of the saints in this chapter, by St. Francis de Sales, St. Teresa of Avila, or St. Bonaventure, and explain what it tells you about the Eucharist.

Name:_____

Death

Answer the following questions in complete sentences.

1. Why must we die?

2. Explain the phrase: "death is not the end of life, but only the end of this life."

3. What does our Faith tell us about death? Since we know death will come to all of us, what should do?

Name:_____

Preparing for Death

Answer the following questions in complete sentences.

1. Explain how the following things can help you to prepare for death.

    The Sacraments of Baptism and Confession:

    The Sacrament of the Holy Eucharist:

    Following God's laws:

    Virtue:

    The Sacrament of the Anointing of the Sick:

2. Why can we have faith and hope?

3. How can we grow and exercise faith and love?

Name:_____

The Particular Judgment

Answer the following questions in complete sentences.

1. Explain the Particular Judgment, including when we face it, how we will see ourselves, and what will happen to our soul afterward.

2. What determines whether we go to heaven, hell, or **purgatory**?

3. If God does not want people to go to hell, why is it possible for us to end up there?

4. Explain how purgatory is an example of God's perfect justice and mercy.

A Happy Death

Write a letter or a prayer to God, praying for the graces necessary for a happy death.

_____

_____

_____

_____

_____

_____

_____

_____

_____

_____

_____

_____

_____

Name:_____

The Second Coming

Answer the following questions in complete sentences.

1. What does the Nicene Creed teach about the Second Coming?

2. Compare Jesus' first coming and his Second Coming.

3. What signs did Jesus tell his disciples would precede the Second Coming? Look up Matthew 24 in your Bible. Even knowing these signs, can we now for sure when the world will end?

4. Should we look forward to the Second Coming? Why or why not?

Name:_____

The General Judgment

Answer the following questions in complete sentences.

1. Who will be judged at the General Judgment?

2. What will be made known?

3. Will there be a need for purgatory? What will happen to the souls there?

4. What will happen to evil?

Name:_____

Resurrection of the Body

Answer the following questions in complete sentences.

1. Will our bodies be reunited with our souls? Why?

2. What does it mean for our bodies to be glorified?

3. What are four properties of the glorified body? Explain them.
    1.

    2.

    3.

    4.

4. What will happen to the earth at the General Judgment?

5. What awaits us after all this comes to pass?

Name:_____

Be Prepared

Read the Bible passages below and explain how each shows us how to be prepared for Jesus' Second Coming.

Matthew 24:36–42, The Need to Be Prepared:

_____

_____

_____

_____

_____

_____

Matthew 25:1–13, The Parable of the Virgins:

_____

_____

_____

_____

_____

_____

Matthew 25:31–26, The Last Judgment:

_____

_____

_____

_____

_____